The day after I was sworn in as a federal judge, Judge Louis Pollak came to visit, tapping on an open door in my new chambers, saying, "May I come in?" He stayed nearly the entire morning. I was enthralled. That was nearly thirty years ago and the commencement (for me) of an extraordinary friendship.

When deciding cases, judges can speak only with other judges, and so for me, and for many other judges, too, Lou was adviser, counselor and sagacious mentor.

Lou Pollak profoundly and joyfully touched many lives. These vignettes from colleagues—lawyers, academics, and judges—give a telling glimpse of this magnificent person.

ANTHONY J. SCIRICA

U.S. Court of Appeals Judge for the Third Circuit

IF THERE IS ANYONE BETTER than Lou Pollak was at teaching by doing, whether lessons for law or lessons for life, I have not met that person. To be sure, the subtlety and suppleness of his mind—and his delight in the fabric of human experience—were such that learning lessons for law sometimes required patience. There was no wait, however, to receive lessons for life, if only one could learn them. The opportunity to know, let alone to work with, a person so deeply considerate of others, so thoroughly indifferent to hierarchy, and so (quietly) passionate about equal opportunity, was a priceless gift.

Although Lou had helped to hire me as the University of Pennsylvania's first in-house general counsel, we did not get to know each other well until we worked on the *amicus curiae* brief that Penn and a number of other universities filed to assist the Supreme Court in *Regents of the University of California v. Bakke*. The idea that there should be such a brief was Lou's. Fearful that the Court's decision in a case involving admission to a public university might deprive private universities of the freedom to take into account personal characteristics they reasonably deemed important to their educational missions, he took the initiative to persuade me and Penn's president, Martin Meyerson, that Penn should take the lead.

Once we agreed and had put together the group of universities and determined who would be speaking for them, the fun began. The issues were difficult, important, and at times contentious. Lou's contributions to the brief as one of its two primary authors included not just the fruits of deep knowledge of the Constitution, of the struggle for racial equality, and of the role of universities in American society. He had the capacity to win an argument without seeming to argue—deftly employing humor—which made internal divisions about strategy or language much easier to resolve. Thus, when we were searching for language that would describe the freedom we sought to preserve and not be inflammatory, the general counsel of another university suggested the formula used in an earlier brief, "according favorable weight to minority status." One of the two primary authors responded, "That's fine so long as we drop a footnote."[1] The author in question was Al Rosenthal of Columbia, but the technique was as much Lou's as Al's.

Lou's sweet reason was not to be confused with a faint heart, as those who sought to prevent the University of Pennsylvania from filing the brief learned at a meeting of the University Council at which a draft was discussed. Calmly but forcefully rebutting the opponents' arguments, Lou's advocacy won the day. The brief was filed, and it featured prominently in Justice Powell's pivotal opinion in *Bakke*. In giving Lou some of the credit for helping tens of thousands of young people to benefit from the institutional freedom thus preserved, let us also remember those whose lives he changed simply by the power of example.

STEPHEN B. BURBANK

David Berger Professor for the Administration of Justice
University of Pennsylvania Law School

FORSAN ET HAEC OLIM MEMINISSE JUVABIT: Virgil's *Aeneid* begins with those words—"Someday, perhaps, this too will seem worth remembering." When, only a few days ago, Kathy asked me to speak, she told me she had forgotten about Yale. In a way it is *singularly* appropriate that Yale should have been forgotten, and *trivially* appropriate, that I should be the one to bring it back to mind today. The latter because, for my sins, I have spent a considerable time trying to make Yale Law School worth remembering. The former, for deeper reasons involving Lou and what needs to be said in his memory . . . memory, that word again.

Today, I do not wish to speak of Lou as a teacher. I spoke of that a while ago when his portrait was presented here [in the ceremonial courtroom of the U. S. Federal Courthouse, Philadelphia], and what, in that role, he meant to me and to so many, and how—with good reason—I choose to teach under another portrait of his. Nor will I speak of what Lou has meant to all of us, and again to me in particular,

1 "Hereinafter referred to as 'It.'"

as a judge . . . as a *really* great judge. Rather, I will talk of the period that Lou himself, at times, wanted to forget . . . his deanship at Yale. For indeed, as the poet said, *this too* is well worth remembering.

Lou became dean at Yale in 1965. That year we thought that the good battles had all been won. Integration, we believed, had taken hold and—following on the martyrdom of President Kennedy and the election of 1964—would continue to proceed apace. The graduating class of 1966—at Yale Law School—Lou's first year as dean, had a fair number of African Americans in it. I recall those in my Torts class, and, this is the odd thing, *in that first year class* they were seen not as black, but as epitomes of *the colleges* they had gone to. John Rose, looking as if he had skied in from Dartmouth; Dave Pitinsky, the perfect New Yorker from Columbia; Drew Days, the classic, from a good small college—Hamilton; Hugh Price, the elegant Williams man; and, perhaps most eminently, Haywood Burns, from Harvard, with one book already under his belt. Clearly integration had worked and the great society was near at hand.

Oh, yes, the prophet in the person of Charlie Reich was walking the halls, saying, "Repent for the end of the world is near." But who believed him? And then it all came apart. Was it Vietnam? Was it the realization that what had been achieved was meager, and what still needed to be done monstrously hard? I don't know. It is a fact that each of those first-year students I mentioned became significant leaders in the struggle that still lay ahead. And an important part of that struggle occurred immediately in the law school.

Times of change, times of struggle, are always difficult. Some abhor them—Lou's successor as dean, so incorrectly, so sadly, called those days "the dark ages." Faculty left Harvard; faculty at Yale did not leave, but many tried to hide in their offices or at home. Lou, instead, saw that these were times that demanded strong and yet immensely subtle leadership. He saw that much for the better could *now* be done and that it *could* be done precisely because there was an almost revolutionary demand for change. He also saw that this had to be done without losing the things, and the people, from the past that deserved keeping.

And so it happened. African Americans were sought out and came to Yale in larger numbers than ever before. More important, unlike those I mentioned earlier, they came not from the great private colleges, and from already middle class origins. Rather, they brought with them far more diverse, and often more troublesome, backgrounds. And, with their coming, ways of teaching, rules of governance, intra-faculty relationships all changed—never to return.

It was inevitable that the dean who oversaw that time should have been attacked by those who sought the changes . . . for not doing more, and faster. In time, however, they, better than anyone, recognized how truly great Lou's achievements were. Today, those Lou brought to the school *and protected* there, whether they are sitting on U.S. Courts of Appeals, in Congress, or on law faculties, or are still in the trenches, remember him as the one who made it possible.

It was also inevitable that those who were frightened by the changes should have blamed the dean for not being a twentieth-century Radetzky destroying these modern 1848ers. Later, though, even these—perhaps less consciously and certainly less verbally than those who had sought change—came to rely on, and almost to rejoice in, the very changes that they so bitterly opposed. I was a kid then—on the faculty, but still a kid. And so I was neither one of the students ferociously seeking a better world and a better school, nor was I one of those whose way of living and teaching seemed threatened by the demands. I could watch the masterful way in which Lou handled that most difficult and wonderful—full of wonders and of problems—time. And I stored it in my memory.

Now, some forty-five years later, and having been a dean myself in far easier days, I call forth those memories and can say honestly and happily, "This was a great, great dean. No one else I have known could have done as much, and as well." I, like so many here, loved and honored Lou as a teacher and friend and I, again like so many here, loved and respected Lou as a judge. But Lou's accomplishments as dean at Yale, like the story of Aeneas that led ultimately to Rome, and to a grander Troy, also deserve the highest possible honor and respect. They are truly worth remembering.[2]

GUIDO CALABRESI

Former Dean
Sterling Professor of Law Emeritus
Professional Lecturer
Yale Law School
Circuit Judge
United States Court of Appeals for the Second Circuit

IT IS A WELL-KNOWN REALITY that all judges appointed under Article III, § 1 of the United States Constitution are appointed by the president and confirmed "with the Advice and Consent of the Senate."[3] With the making of all Article III judges in the hands of the executive

2 These remarks were delivered at the memorial service for Judge Pollak on 12 June 2012.
3 U.S. Const. Art. II, §2.

and the Senate, it is no surprise that the paths to such judgeships can vary widely.

In this respect, it is useful to compare the paths of two judges appointed within months of each other in 1978, Richard S. Arnold and Louis H. Pollak. We know the exact route of Judge Arnold's path because he was always quite frank about it. His account of how his path began is instructive, and so I reproduce it in Judge Arnold's own words:

> "Some judges (you may not believe this) are political appointees, but I was appointed on merit. My merit was that I worked for a United States Senator. One day in 1978, as I was working for Senator Dale Bumpers of Arkansas, word came that a vacancy had occurred on the District Court in Little Rock. A few days later, the Senator called me into his office, and he said, 'Richard, fix up a letter to the President recommending you to be United States District Judge.' So I wrote him a hell of a letter—the finest, most fulsome, most eloquent letter of recommendation ever sent by a United States Senator."[4]

Even more vivid is Judge Arnold's account of the end of his path after President Carter nominated him for the district court bench in Arkansas.

> And so, one day when Senator Bumpers and I got on the elevator in the Dirksen Senate Office Building, who should come on with us but the powerful—the name and title of this man were never repeated without the adjective "powerful"—the powerful James O. Eastland, chairman of the Senate Judiciary Committee. And so we got on the elevator and Dale said, "Jim, Richard here"—and he jerked his thumb at me, as if at an insignificant object (which I was)—"Richard here has been nominated to be District Judge, and I want you to confirm him." And Senator [Eastland] looked at him, and he said, "Whatever you say, Dale." Then we got down to the bottom of the building and it was time to get off of the elevator. The doors opened up, and Eastland looked at me and said, "After you, Judge." So I got confirmed in the elevator.[5]

I'll refer here to Judge Arnold's description of his first judicial path as "the Arnold Route."[6] Judge Pollak's path to his district court judgeship bore no point of congruency with the Arnold Route, although, in the end, there came a modest convergence.

---

4 Richard S. Arnold, "The Federal Courts: Causes of Discontent," 56 *SMU L. Rev.* 767 (2003).

5 Id. 767–68.

6 It bears noting that notwithstanding his oft-incanted confession, Judge Arnold then went on to become a most respected judge of the United States Court of Appeals for the Eighth Circuit (indeed became its chief judge) and served with distinction until his death in 2004. See Neil A. Lewis, "Richard S. Arnold, 68, Judge Once Eyed for Supreme Court, Dies," New York Times, 25 Sept. 2004.

As many are aware, Judge Pollak was primarily a scholar after he finished his clerkship with Supreme Court Justice Rutledge in 1949 and got two years as an associate in a major New York law firm, Paul, Weiss, behind him. While on the faculty of Yale Law School, first as a professor and later dean, Professor Pollak published the two-volume *The Constitution and the Supreme Court: A Documentary History* in 1966. He later became a professor and dean at the University of Pennsylvania Law School for three years, ending with his judicial appointment in 1978.

To be sure, Louis H. Pollak, Esquire, had a notable, if brief, courtroom career, most consequentially as part of the NAACP legal team that ultimately triumphed in *Brown v. Board of Education.*[7] Lawyer Pollak also had some litigation experience while an associate at Paul, Weiss, but he was, as he would be the first to say, primarily an academic. Although he came to know most, if not all, of the Supreme Court justices in his academic career, he had no political patron like Senator Bumpers.

But as it turned out, the then new junior senator from Pennsylvania, H. John Heinz III, had made a campaign promise in his successful 1976 campaign that his first act as senator would be to create, with then-senior senator Richard Schweiker, a Merit Selection Commission to vet candidates for vacancies on the three Pennsylvania federal district courts. And thus shortly after taking office, Senator Heinz, with Senator Schweiker's support, formed that commission, and I suggested certain members for it. Senator Heinz agreed that the Secretary of the commission should be my senior partner, Lewis H. Van Dusen, Jr.

So in 1978, when a vacancy occurred on the Eastern District of Pennsylvania court, I asked Lew Van Dusen who some of the candidates were. To my surprise, the first name Lew mentioned to me was Louis Pollak. This was amazingly good news, a view Lew Van Dusen shared. So it wasn't long before Dean Pollak was among the handful of names recommended to the two Senators.

Although John Heinz was not legally trained (he was a mere graduate of Yale College and Harvard Business School), he regarded the federal courts with a certain awe. He was, in fact, anything but cynical about the subject and often said that the recommendation of district court judgeships was among the most important things United States Senators do. I therefore knew that when John would ask me about Dean Pollak this would be an easy sale, and it most assuredly was. After I recounted to John Lou's work on *Brown* and his deanships

7 347 U.S. 483 (1954).

at Yale and Penn, he said to me words that, in sum, amounted to, "Well, this is a no-brainer, isn't it?" I agreed that it was hardly a tough call, and the rest became the distinguished career of United States District Judge Louis H. Pollak.

And what a career it was! A measure of the regard Judge Pollak enjoyed may be found in the many law clerks he sent to the Supreme Court for clerkships with, for example, Justice Brennan and, later, Justice Souter. And as a trial judge, Lou never lost the grace that he demonstrated as dean of two major law schools. This explains why lawyers all gave him their utmost respect and, dare I say, affection. The judgeship never went to his head.

And Judge Pollak also never lost his scholar's sensitivity and attentiveness to history. I was not long ago put in mind of this while reading Walter Isaacson's magnificent biography of the Founder of the American Philosophical Society. I was particularly struck by Franklin's words in opposition to the high-handedness of the then proprietor of Pennsylvania, words that could readily have come from Judge Pollak's pen or mouth if he were with us today: "Those who would give up essential liberty to purchase a little temporary safety deserve neither liberty nor safety."[8]

These were words and a perspective that Judge Pollak brought to life every day in his courtroom.

STEWART DALZELL[9]

United States District Judge for the Eastern District of Pennsylvania

LOU POLLAK WAS A MAGNIFICENT JUDGE, a distinguished constitutional scholar, an inspiring teacher, and twice a beloved law school dean. Such diverse accomplishments don't usually come neatly tied in a single package. But in Lou's case it was all of a piece—the achievements emerged out of his deep humanity and quiet personal connection with almost everyone with whom he came into contact. He was a serial mensch—and it brought out the best in people around him.

I first met Lou more than thirty-five years ago when we both arrived in the U. S. Federal Courthouse in Philadelphia, reporting for duty, as it were. To say that there was a difference in our positions is the understatement of the year. I was bright eyed and bushy tailed, fresh

8 Walter Isaacson, *Benjamin Franklin* (2004 edition), 169.

9 Judge Dalzell served as a colleague and friend of Judge Pollak's for more than twenty years.

out of law school, beginning service as a law clerk to the Honorable Leon Higginbotham.

Lou had just stepped down from the Penn Law deanship, having served on both the Penn and Yale law faculties, where he had also been dean, and was then the newest member of the federal bench.

To a star-struck fledging attorney such as myself, Lou was a legend.

Judge Higginbotham, his close friend, let the clerks know that this icon would be coming to the chambers, and he would introduce us. We all knew Lou's background—his co-authorship of the brief in *Brown*, the constitutional scholarship, and his renowned civil rights and civil liberties advocacy.

I was prepared—literally—to quake in his presence. Yet when he entered the room, with that warm avuncular smile and soft blue eyes connecting with everyone in his presence, I was immediately overcome by the Pollak effect, as I would be the remainder of my life.

He wanted to know all about me—who I was—and what had I done that had led me to that point in my career. And he then congratulated me for having the privilege of clerking for my soon-to-be mentor, Judge Higginbotham. In short, from the first moment, he related to me in a very special and personal way that I will never forget.

And that human connection was really no different when I was a law clerk, when I joined the Penn Law faculty years later, or when I assumed his former position as dean of Penn Law. For Lou, it was always about the individual, regardless of role.

Indeed, one of the most vivid moments when I saw those qualities on display was several years ago when Lou's judicial portrait was unveiled. Just as when his dean's portrait was unveiled years earlier at Penn, after the presentations he went around the room and made a sincere, personal observation about almost everyone present, explaining their relationship to him and the issues and people they all held dear.

That was one of the vital sources of his greatness. He loved humanity in the abstract and in the particular—and for Lou, the two were inextricably linked. Those qualities undoubtedly help to explain why the Penn Law faculty strong-armed him to become dean.

Let me be clear—I, of all people, understand why someone would need to be coerced to be a law dean, but why the faculty would focus on Lou of all the people in the world to apply that pressure should be obvious to anyone who knew him. His ability to relate to people brought out the best in others and made him a force for an institution's and society's good.

The faculty wanted to be at a place led by Lou and to do their best work with Lou as dean. He inspired and supported their best instincts. He embodied the culture and values they held dear.

In that regard, I am proud to be one of Lou's thousands of academic friends and admirers. He had so many friends at Penn Law School alone, but I must make special note of three, who for purposes of anonymity, as Lou would put it, might be referred to as Clyde Summers, his lifelong academic soul mate, who accompanied him from Yale to Penn; the intellectually intense Frank Goodman; and civil procedure guru Stephen Burbank. All three remained close to Kathy and Lou for life.

The Penn Law community, which welcomed Lou in 1975, will always be grateful that, after his arm was twisted to become dean, he never let us go. He remained on the faculty and deeply involved with the law school for thirty years after joining the bench.

He even won the teaching award the last year he taught at the school before his health prevented him from continuing to serve. And, as a fitting capstone, the law school's public service award was named in his honor a month before his death, an honor for which he expressed deep pride in the last conversation I had with him.

Of course, if Lou were giving a tribute to a colleague, he would continue far longer than I will be permitted. That was Lou.

I remember when he gave a public tribute to Professor Bob Gorman at Bob's retirement dinner many years ago. I had been dean for less than a month and did not adequately appreciate the full extent of Lou's passion for speaking at length about justice—and people. Lou opened his remarks by saying, "I've been asked by Mike to talk for ten minutes." And then he laughed, ceremoniously ripped up some papers he had carried to the podium—presumably including my invitation—and with that trademark mischievous smile of his, launched into a thirty-minute address.

Based on this history, I thought I had taken adequate precautions several years later when I asked Lou to speak for ten minutes to our entering class at orientation about the role of the Supreme Court. I repeated the time limitations in a letter, and on the day of the event called to remind him a third time, "Lou, ten minutes." He laughed, and said, "Of course, Mike."

Well, he spoke for forty-five minutes that day about the history of the Supreme Court, beginning with *Marbury v. Madison*, and detailing the Court's great successes and failures over the full sweep of history.

It was a tour de force—though a forty-five-minute tour de force. The students didn't get their dinner on time, but they did get a lesson that would last a lifetime. Indeed, one remarked to me recently that it was her most memorable experience in law school. In retrospect, I have to wonder how I ever thought I could place a time limitation on Lou. Or should.

When Lou relinquished his deanship to become a district court judge, the editors of the *University of Pennsylvania Law Review* dedicated an issue in his honor. They noted that "[t]he entire law school community will miss his gentle presence as dean, especially those who have been fortunate enough to have been his students." And they offered this prescient prediction: "The qualities that made Dean Pollak's tenure at this law school memorable will continue to serve him well as a federal judge."

At the time not everyone was so sanguine. As my fellow dean Bob Mundheim recollected recently, "Lou had been an appellate advocate, not a trial lawyer, and many wondered whether this person who tended to listen, had enormous patience, who did not direct directly, they wondered would he be able to run a courtroom? Would cases go on forever?" Indeed, Bob confessed that he would have bet against Lou's being a successful trial court judge.

But as Bob later recognized, he was wrong. Lou's greatness was of a piece, and his ability to connect with people across the board ultimately made him a superb trial court judge, understanding counsel and parties alike, just as it made him a remarkable dean and teacher.

It is with his role as a teacher that I would conclude my comments.

His students adored him. "I will still be telling stories about him fifty years from now," one said after taking his seminar.

Another former student, to whom I will give the final word, perhaps summed it up best when commenting at the end of what turned out to be the last class Lou ever taught. The student wrote, "The world would be a far better place if all men—and women—were more like Judge Pollak. What a wonderful, wonderful man. What an inspiration for everyone around him."[10]

MICHAEL A. FITTS

President
Tulane University
Former Dean and Bernard G. Segal Professor of Law
University of Pennsylvania Law School

WHEN I WAS VERY YOUNG, my grandfather told me that any consideration of a man's contributions to his fellow man should begin with

10 These remarks were delivered at the U.S. Federal Courthouse in Philadelphia on 28 September 2012.

a brief summary of the services he had rendered to the Episcopal Church, the Republican Party, and the Harvard football team. He called this "justification by works."

I had this instruction in mind in the summer of 1976 when—in my first days as an associate editor of the *University of Pennsylvania Law Review*—I was told to edit a brief tribute to William Henry Hastie penned by the dean of our law school, Louis H. Pollak. I should add that that tribute (which may be found at 125 *U. Pa. L. Rev.*, p. 1) pretty much defied editing. Indeed, my only contribution—the addition of a single letter to the text the Dean had provided—was quickly rejected by the editor-in-chief on the ground that the author did not spell his name with a "c." Which goes to show that sometimes a law review editor does cave in to an author's whim.

Anyway, the first two sentences of Pollak's essay may bear re-reading: "By the time he died," Pollak wrote, "William Henry Hastie had been a great judge—indeed, one of the most distinguished judges in the nation—for a long time. So long a time (twenty-six years) that it is not easy to remember that he was a major force in the law years before he became Judge Hastie."

All of which could now be said about Pollak himself, who ended up serving even longer as "one of the most distinguished judges in the nation."

In any event, back in 1976, Pollak, when contemplating Hastie, said nothing about any of the good works my grandfather had valued. He chose instead to praise his subject's "intellectual power" and "unflagging energy." And he put particular emphasis on Judge Hastie's "unremitting commitment to principle." All of which is what my grandfather would have called "justification by faith."

Now the fact is that in the many years since I first read Pollak's unedited tribute to Hastie, I had ample opportunity to observe both Pollak's works and Pollak's faith, as it were, and I believe I could provide a stirring justification of him on either ground. But I'm not sure that is what is wanted. So permit me, instead, to provide a few quick sketches of the man himself.

Picture him, if you will, at an Inn of Court dinner sometime around the turn of the millennium. He has reluctantly agreed to give the after-dinner talk, but instead of tiring his audience with something earnest, he is telling us a bit about the practice of law in New York a generation or two ago. It is a subject about which he knows a fair amount, having made the obviously prudent decision to marry the boss's daughter while working at Paul, Weiss in the early 1950s. And as he talks, Pollak unwittingly gives us glimpses of his own roots. He recalls his mother-in-law, who was a kind yet energetic woman, the kind of person my grandfather would have called a "do-gooder." And his father-in-law, Louis Weiss, who was one of the leading lawyers of his time and a founder of Paul, Weiss. Weiss was the kind of person my grandfather would have called a "gentleman."

And then Pollak is holding up a photograph of the lawyers of Sullivan & Cromwell circa 1912—a photograph that included his father, Walter Pollak, who was the kind of person my grandfather would have called a "Bolshevik." Rather than staying with a perfectly respectable firm—as Sullivan & Cromwell then was—the elder Pollak had gone on to make his name representing the less respectable. He was also the inventor of the constitutional doctrine of incorporation, having successfully pedaled that counterintuitive idea to the Supreme Court while losing a case called *Gitlow v. New York*. I cite the case now only for the proposition that the later Pollak's constitutional views were probably genetically fixed and thus not entirely his fault.

But enough of Pollak's heritage, however much it may have influenced him. Let us picture him, instead, teaching a class on federal courts in the early spring of 1978. Most of the students are "third years" who already have their jobs or clerkships and who are playing out the string, as it were. The dean, as he then was, is doing what he can to engage these unengageable students in a discussion of *Louisville and Nashville Railroad v. Mottley*, 211 U.S. 149 (1908). He is employing his own version of the Socratic method—which is far too gentle to inspire the fear that makes the Socratic method effective. Accordingly, with this group, his questions are producing responses like, "Gee, I don't know" or "Sorry, I didn't read the assignment."

If the dean is annoyed or disappointed—as he could have been—he gives no sign of it. Instead, he reacts to each response with a kindly if somewhat quizzical smile and then presses on with another question—all in the hope that he might be able to teach even this class something about the well-pleaded complaint. He will fail at this. But a couple of the students sitting toward the back of the class marvel nonetheless at how patiently and gracefully he persists in what seems to them a pointless exercise. They conclude that that is just the way he is. By which they mean, it is his character. Years later, they will think that lessons in character matter more than the facts of the *Mottley* case.

But maybe that picture is a little too academic. Perhaps it would be better to depict an insurance coverage case tried to a jury in June of 1987. And maybe the plaintiff's lawyer keeps changing his theories—and the defendant's lawyer keeps asking the same questions—and maybe there's an expert on Mexican law answering every question, "Yes," no matter what it is, because his only experience of an American courtroom comes from television and he thinks the lawyers will be able to destroy him on cross-examination unless he agrees with whatever they say on direct.

And maybe the trial goes seven days and isn't ultimately about anything all that important—although God knows we all thought it was. But the judge is acting throughout as if all the lawyers and all the witnesses and even the jurors were real people with real lives, as if they actually mattered. So he treats all of them courteously all of the time. No matter what. Even that confused and frightened expert from Mexico City. It might even be said—indeed, it is said—that this judge suffers fools gladly—or, if not gladly, then more than he should. Yet at the end of the trial, none of the participants feels incompetent or foolish—even though all of them were at times. Which was probably the judge's principal contribution to the festivities. The kind of contribution that counts for little in the world of great works and for even less in the world of lofty principles.

But most of us don't actually live in those worlds. We live in this one. And when we live in it long enough, we grow less impressed with the works of men and we start to wonder about "unremitting commitment to principle" even when we can agree on the principle, which we cannot always do. So sometimes we remember an older and different teaching—that a man is not justified either by his works or by his faith. That is only done—if it is done at all—by something called grace.

And grace is an uncommon phenomenon that we do not often encounter and cannot easily explain. Which is why we call it a gift. An inward and invisible gift that is nonetheless manifested by countless outward and visible signs. And as surprising as it is to see it, the fact is that all of us know it when we do. And could not miss it in Lou.[11]

ALFRED W. PUTNAM, JR.

Partner, Drinker Biddle & Reath

IT IS A PRIVILEGE to write in memory of Judge Louis H. Pollak. I shall refer to him as Lou, because the only time he reproved me—gently—was when I addressed him as "Judge Pollak." Others are more qualified to write in Lou's honor: those who knew him when Thurgood Marshall first recruited him to volunteer for the NAACP Legal Defense and Educational Fund; or when he worked on the NAACP team that briefed *Brown v. Board of Education*; or at Yale Law School when Lou was a professor and then the dean; or at Penn Law School when Lou

11 This tribute is an edited version of remarks given at the unveiling of Judge Pollak's portrait at the United States Courthouse in Philadelphia on 21 May 2010.

was our dean; or during Lou's many years on the bench in the Eastern District of Pennsylvania. But perhaps I can speak for more than a decade's worth of our Penn Law students, including some who had the opportunity to serve in Lou's chambers as interns or law clerks, and others who learned from him in his seminar on Great Supreme Court Cases, and all of whom revered and loved him.

As a reporter to the committee that drafts model jury instructions for use in civil cases in the Third Circuit—a committee on which Lou served since its inception—I came to know both his deep wisdom and his equally deep kindness. The model instructions can be added to many other features of American law that are more just because of Lou's work. And when I walk through the lobby of the courthouse at Sixth and Market Streets, I remember Lou, already in his eighties at that point, walking me out of the courthouse and onto Market Street so that he could hail me a cab because I had a broken foot.

Everyone who knew Lou will recognize that quality. He was not merely a great academic, lawyer, and judge. He was a husband and father devoted to his family. He was a judge who decided a fair housing case involving a challenge to the siting of a homeless shelter and then—after the case was over—walked unrecognized through the shelter so that he could see how it had turned out. He was a judge who was interested in the well-being of a litigant many years after her case had gone to judgment.

Lou helped to shape the great concepts of justice in twentieth-century American law, but those concepts were not abstractions to him. Each human being whom he encountered received his attention and concern.

Elected 2000: Councilor 2004–10; Committees: Meetings 2000–09; Membership V 2002–08; Phillips Prize 2002–11

CATHERINE STRUVE
Professor of Law
University of Pennsylvania Law School

Lou Pollak: The Road to *Brown v. Board of Education* and Beyond

LEANNA LEE WHITMAN
Retired Research Librarian/Archivist
Third Circuit Court of Appeals

MICHAEL HAYES
Librarian, Wilmington, Delaware Branch
Third Circuit Court of Appeals

Books dominated each room in District Court Judge Louis H. Pollak's private chambers. Whether crammed on shelves, piled on top of chairs, or mixed together with briefs, law journals, and papers and stacked on top of desks and tables—they ruled. The chambers, located on the sixteenth floor of the federal courthouse in Philadelphia, gave the judge a panoramic view of the National Constitution Center and beyond to the Delaware River and the outer limits of the city. Along with this view, when he looked up from his work, Pollak liked gazing at dozens of photographs of family and clerks that he propped together in clusters; alongside these groupings stood a photo of Bobby Kennedy, signed by his widow, Ethel.

Louis Pollak was an esteemed legal scholar when he was appointed to the bench of the U.S. District Court, Eastern District of Pennsylvania, in 1978; he had served as dean of Yale Law School from 1965 to 1970 and dean of the University of Pennsylvania Law School from 1975 to 1978. Consequently, he came to the court with ingrained scholarly habits. He maintained an impressive list of academic publications, read voraciously, and enjoyed perusing the collections of the court library after hours. At the same time, in an extension of his life-long fascination with Abraham Lincoln, for several years Pollak re-read close to a dozen times a biography of Lincoln's attorney general, Edward Bates, and Bates's diary from 1859 to 1866.

Judge Pollak served the court for thirty-four years, from 1978 until his death on 8 May 2012. Stemming from his work on the landmark civil rights case *Brown v. Board of Education,*[1] he was sometimes referred to in the court family as the "living history judge" or the "civil rights judge." Extremely modest by nature, however, Judge Pollak deflected in-depth interviews about his involvement with *Brown* with a self-deprecating question: "Do you think anybody would be interested?"

A few years ago, Judge Pollak finally submitted to a series of oral interviews with me. And so as we looked out over the National Constitutional Center on a bright fall day, Judge Pollak turned and graciously offered me a seat in a Victorian chair while he took his father's overstuffed chair. He started off: "Before we begin, let me tell you about the chair that you are sitting in. It belonged to Kathy's [his wife Katherine Weiss Pollak] grandfather, Dr. Sigmund Pollitzer, a prominent dermatologist who was born in the U.S. in the mid-1850s but had to go to Germany to get a medical education because of the extraordinary difficulty Jews had in getting into medical schools in this country at the time. Kathy's grandmother gave it to us as a wedding present."[2] We had agreed that Judge Pollak would discuss *Brown* from his perspective first as a young volunteer in Thurgood Marshall's brain trust and then as author of the summary of argument (synopsis) of the *Brown* brief. He would try to imagine a camera mounted on his shoulders, and with it he would move in for close-ups and pull back for sweeping shots.

Louis (Lou) Heilprin Pollak was born in New York City on 7 December 1922 to Walter Heilprin Pollak (1887–1940) and Marion Heilprin (who were second cousins). Walter Pollak was born in Summit, New Jersey, into a family of bookish, nonreligious Jews who had immigrated to the United States from Poland in the mid-1830s.[3] He graduated from Harvard in 1907 and from Harvard Law School in 1910, and went on to become a famed litigator and civil libertarian.

When Lou Pollak was a toddler, his father, a lawyer for the American Civil Liberties Union (ACLU), took on the landmark case *Gitlow v. New York* (268 U.S. 652 [1925]). Benjamin Gitlow, a leader of the left-wing section of the Socialist party, had been arrested, tried, and found

1 *Brown v. Board of Education*, 347 U.S. 483 (1954).

2 According to Katherine Weiss Pollak (Kathy), the author was sitting in a Morris chair, an early type of reclining chair that was adapted from a design by William Morris, a leader of the Arts and Crafts movement.

3 Louis H. Pollak in *The Yale Biographical Dictionary of American Law,* ed. Roger K. Newman, 430 (2009).

guilty under the New York Criminal Anarchy Law of 1902 for writing, publishing, and distributing a sixteen-page manifesto advocating revolution.

In 1923 in the stately, semicircular Old Senate Chamber, Walter Pollak rose to argue *Gitlow*, his first oral argument before the Supreme Court: "If it pleases the Court: considering the enormity and complexity of this case, I would like to request an additional fifteen minutes to my allotted time of one hour for argument." Chief Justice William Howard Taft turned to his right, to the senior associate justice, Oliver Wendell Holmes, for advice. Holmes leaned over to the chief justice and in an echoing whisper snapped, "I'll see him in hell first!"[4]

Pollak lost *Gitlow*, but according to *The Oxford Companion to the Supreme Court*, "The landmark *Gitlow* case marks the beginning of the 'incorporation' of the First Amendment as a limitation on the states."[5] Pollak argued that the First Amendment's freedom of speech and freedom of press civil liberties were binding not only on the federal government but on individual states as well. He contended that the implicit meaning of liberty in the Fourteenth Amendment ("nor shall any State deprive any person of life, liberty, or property without due process of law") included or "incorporated" rights that were explicitly stated in the First Amendment. The Supreme Court in its opinion stated, "For present purposes we may and do assume that freedom of speech and of the press—which are protected by the First Amendment from abridgement by Congress—are among the fundamental personal rights and 'liberties' protected by the due process clause of the Fourteenth Amendment from impairment by the States."[6] However, although the court accepted Pollak's argument, it ruled that it did not apply in the instant case, and found against *Gitlow*.

Using *Gitlow* as case authority for the incorporation doctrine, Walter Pollak argued twice in the Supreme Court on behalf of the "Scottsboro Boys," first in 1932—(*Powell v. Alabama*, 287 U.S. 45 (1932)), and again in 1935—*Norris v. Alabama*, 294 U.S. 587 (1935). In these cases, nine young black men were arrested in Scottsboro, Alabama, and were charged with raping two white women on a freight train. In *Powell*, Walter Pollak persuaded the Supreme Court to quash the defendants' death sentences because the state had not fulfilled its due process obligation to ensure that the court-appointed counsel

4 Louis H. Pollak, "Walter H. Pollak and the Scottsboro Boys" (panel discussion, Scottsboro Boys, Philadelphia Theatre Company, Suzanne Roberts Theater, Philadelphia, Pa., 15 February 2012).

5 Kermit L. Hall, ed., *The Oxford Companion to the Supreme Court of the United States* (New York and Oxford: Oxford University Press, 1992), 339.

6 *Gitlow v. New York*, 268 U.S. at 666.

competently represented indigent and unlettered defendants. He persuaded the Supreme Court, in *Norris*, to quash the defendants' death sentences because blacks had been systematically excluded from grand and petit juries in Alabama, resulting in a denial of equal protection. These cases marked the beginning of the Court's intensive constitutional surveillance of the state criminal process.[7] Summarizing the Scottsboro cases, Lou Pollak said, "My father not only saved the lives of the men, but he made new constitutional law."[8]

Walter Pollak's persuasive prowess in his own home, however, was far less evident. Lou was ten years old when his father argued *Powell*, thirteen years old when his father argued *Norris*. He did not attend either Supreme Court argument and had only a vague notion of his father's work.[9] For his part, Walter was concerned about Lou's poor reading habits, so he drew up a required reading list that included a book on constitutional law. The only thing that the son remembered was that he found the book neither very good nor interesting.[10]

Nonetheless, Louis Pollak absorbed a passion to defend the right to dissent and the right to be treated fairly and equally under law—grants made by the Constitution. He entered Harvard College in the fall of 1940. In April 1941 the *Harvard Crimson* reported a student protest against two bills in the Massachusetts legislature that would have removed from the ballot the Communist Party and any other groups advocating forceful overthrow of the government: "Louis H. Pollak '44 said in a statement released by the delegation last night, 'This bill is designed to protect our citizenry from "un-American" doctrines by barring the Communist Party from the ballot. But is not the very basis of democracy the belief that no ideal is absolute, and no body of men capable of absolute definition of Americanism!'"[11]

Pollak graduated from Harvard in May 1943 with a bachelor of arts degree in history and literature, magna cum laude in field, and Phi Beta Kappa honors. Right after graduation he served in the U.S. Army and was stationed near Washington, D.C., where he thought he might be able to begin law school. Pursuing this idea, he went to Howard

---

7 Louis H. Pollak in *The Yale Biographical Dictionary of American Law* at 430.

8 Louis H. Pollak, discussion with Leanna Lee Whitman, September 2010.

9 In later years, Lou Pollak reviewed his father's briefs for *Gitlow* and the Scottsboro Boys cases, and agreed with legal scholars that Walter Pollak was a brilliant lawyer. But Lou points out that his father's writing had a major flaw: Walter thought the combination of a comma/dash (",--") was an acceptable form of punctuation. Louis H. Pollak, "Walter H. Pollak and the Scottsboro Boys" (panel discussion, Scottsboro Boys).

10 Louis H. Pollak, interview with Leanna Lee Whitman, 1 November 2011.

11 "H.L.U. Forced Protest Communist Ballot-Cut," *Harvard Crimson*, 15 April 1941.

Law School, part of one of the oldest historically black universities in the United States. He assumed that the place to obtain information was the Office of the Dean. He was received there cordially by a slender, quiet man of about forty, who listened thoughtfully. After completing a somewhat jumbled statement of his plan, Pollak paused. An awkward silence followed. Dean William Hastie quickly stepped in: "It's all right, Mr. Pollak, we accept whites."[12] Pollak was deeply impressed with the willingness of Howard to accept whites and with Hastie's gracious manner, especially after considering the history between the races in this country.[13]

However, Pollak decided to enroll in Yale Law School after he completed his military service. He graduated in 1948, editor-in-chief of the *Yale Law Journal*. He then clerked for United States Supreme Court Justice Wiley B. Rutledge. Also in the 1948–49 term, Justice Felix Frankfurter hired William (Bill) T. Coleman as the Supreme Court's first African American law clerk.[14] During their clerkship year, Pollak and Bill Coleman began an enduring friendship.

After their year at the Court ended, Pollak found employment with the New York law firm of Paul, Weiss, Rifkind, Wharton & Garrison, a high-powered liberal law firm that was the only interfaith Wall Street law firm in town.[15] (Louis H. Pollak and Katherine Weiss, daughter of Louis Weiss—a founder of Paul, Weiss—were married in 1952.)

Bill Coleman was unable to find a job with any law firm in his hometown of Philadelphia, but Coleman was interviewed and immediately hired by Louis Weiss in the summer of 1949. This made Paul, Weiss the sole interracial, as well as the sole interfaith, Wall Street law firm at the time.[16]

Thurgood Marshall's Brain Trust

Shortly after Pollak and Coleman started at Paul, Weiss, Coleman received a call.

---

12 331 F.3d XXXIV-XXXV; Louis H. Pollak, discussion with Leanna Lee Whitman, September 2010.

13 Louis H. Pollak, discussion with Leanna Lee Whitman, September 2010.

14 Moreover, the previous year, Bill Coleman became the first African American to clerk for a federal appellate judge when he clerked for Judge Herbert F. Goodrich of the U.S. Court of Appeals for the Third Circuit (1947–48); he later became the fourth United States secretary of transportation (1975–77) under President Gerald Ford.

15 Richard Kluger, *Simple Justice: The History of* Brown v. Board of Education *and Black America's Struggle for Equality* (New York: Alfred A. Knopf, 1976), 292. Kluger states that Paul, Weiss was an interfaith and interracial firm before Coleman was hired.

16 Katherine Weiss Pollak, discussion with Leanna Lee Whitman, 14 August 2012.

MARSHALL: Mr. Coleman, good morning. My name is Thurgood Marshall. I am chief counsel of the NAACP Legal Defense and Educational Fund.

COLEMAN: Yes sir, Mr. Marshall. I know who you are. I am a great admirer of your work. We met at the Harvard Law School a few years ago when you were visiting with Mr. Houston and Mr. Hastie. . . .

MARSHALL: Let me get right to the point, Mr. Coleman. Bill Hastie has had some very fine things to say about you. I would like to invite you to a meeting early next month of about twenty-five lawyers to talk strategy. Some of us believe this is the time to bring lawsuits attacking racial segregation head-on in the public schools in the South—kindergarten through twelfth grade. . . . John Davis, from Lincoln University, will also be coming to describe some recent studies on the psychological damage of racial segregation on colored children.[17]

Coleman spoke to partners at Paul, Weiss about Thurgood Marshall's call, and found them to be enthusiastically supportive of Marshall's invitation. Coleman also invited his good friend Pollak to join him. Pollak relished the idea and quickly got permission from the partners at Paul, Weiss to join the quest. Toward the end of his life Pollak would write, "I had the incomparable professional opportunity that has defined the balance of my career: to serve as one of the volunteer lawyers who assisted Thurgood Marshall and his associates of the NAACP Legal Defense Fund in the school segregation cases. . . ."[18]

BACKGROUND: SEPARATE BUT EQUAL

The separate-but-equal doctrine underlying racial segregation became the law of the land in 1896, when the U.S. Supreme Court upheld in *Plessy v. Ferguson* the constitutionality of a Louisiana statute that required railroads to provide "equal but separate accommodations for the white and colored races." Writing for the Court, Associate Justice Henry Billings Brown stated that laws requiring separation of the races did not necessarily imply the inferiority of either race.[19] The Court's reasoning therefore implied that segregation of blacks and whites could nevertheless satisfy the guarantee of equality in the Fourteenth Amendment if both racial groups were treated "equally."

17 William T. Coleman and Donald T. Bliss, *Counsel for the Situation: Shaping the Law to Realize America's Promise* (Washington, D.C.: Brookings Institution Press, 2010), 104.

18 Louis H. Pollak in Mariana Cook, *Justice: Faces of the Human Rights Revolution*, (Bologna: Damiani, 2013), 46.

19 *Plessy v. Ferguson*, 163 U.S. 537, 538 (1896).

In 1929 the National Association for the Advancement of Colored People (NAACP) asked Felix Frankfurter, a member of the NAACP National Legal Committee, for advice in finding a top strategist in the fight against segregation. Frankfurter recommended Charles Houston, the new dean of Howard Law; Houston, in turn, recommended Nathan Margold, a fellow Harvard Law School graduate.[20] So in 1930, the NAACP commissioned Margold to produce a long-range strategic plan to combat racial segregation. Margold focused on public schools in the South. Data gathered by the NAACP showed that in 1930, South Carolina was spending ten times as much on the education of every white child as it was on every black child. Florida, Georgia, Mississippi, and Alabama were spending five times as much. And North Carolina, Maryland, Virginia, Texas, and Oklahoma were spending twice as much.[21] Thus under the *Plessy* separate-but-equal doctrine, public schools in the South were separate-but-egregiously unequal, and therefore susceptible to attack as unconstitutional.

Charles H. Houston

Charles Hamilton Houston, who had graduated class valedictorian at Amherst College in Massachusetts and had been the first black student at Harvard Law School to make Law Review (1921–22), went on to become dean of Howard Law School in 1929. In his five-year tenure, Houston turned a lackluster institution into an accredited and highly respected academic law school. Houston left Howard in 1935 to become special counsel to the NAACP in New York City. He accepted the conclusion of the Margold Report as the best approach to overturning *Plessy*. Houston had traveled widely in the South, investigating and documenting the deplorable state of southern public schools for blacks. However, he felt that the public school systems of the South represented too wide and unwieldy a target. Houston instead decided to begin by inserting a wedge into the system; he would begin with a narrow attack on segregated graduate and professional schools in the South, where often there were no schools that admitted blacks at all, or, if such schools existed, they were extremely inadequate.

At the NAACP, Houston recruited the brightest and most dedicated attorneys to join the mission against racial injustice. Among the outstanding talent to join Houston were William H. Hastie and Thurgood Marshall, whom Houston and Hastie knew from Howard Law School.

---

20 Kluger, *Simple Justice*, 133.

21 Id. at 134.

William H. Hastie

Hastie and Houston, although distant cousins, always considered themselves close family. Hastie followed Houston's footsteps to Amherst College, Harvard Law School, and the *Harvard Law Review*. At Amherst, Hastie graduated class valedictorian; at Harvard Law School, he earned a bachelor of laws degree with honors, and a doctorate in law, and (following Houston) he was the second black law student at Harvard to make *Law Review* (1929–30). Hastie later joined Houston at Howard University Law School, first as a professor and then as dean (1939–46). Founded upon the view that integration is the only rational and intelligent approach to racial justice in America, Houston and Hastie built at Howard Law a curriculum designed to produce a cadre of anti-segregation litigators, "the dry run for lawyers going to the Supreme Court."[22] Richard Kluger's book *Simple Justice* quotes an associate of Houston and Hastie: "Charlie was the philosopher and the architect, and Bill more the legal strategist, linking goals to means."[23]

Thurgood Marshall

Marshall's application to the University of Maryland Law School was rejected because he was black, so he commuted from Baltimore to Howard Law School in Washington, D.C. At Howard, Marshall flourished under the tutelage of Houston and Hastie, graduating first in his class in 1933. By 1936 Marshall was working with his two professors at the NAACP in Baltimore.

NAACP Legal Defense and Educational Fund, Inc.

In 1940, the NAACP created the NAACP Legal Defense and Educational Fund, Inc. (often referred to as the "Inc. Fund" or "LDF") as a separate charitable organization to perform non-propaganda, non-lobbying activities of the NAACP. The LDF became, in practice, the legal arm of the NAACP. Walter White, secretary (the highest executive officer) and CEO of the NAACP, also became secretary of the LDF.[24] White promoted Thurgood Marshall from within the NAACP to chief counsel of the LDF.[25]

22 William H. Hastie, interview with Genna Rae McNeil, 19 September 1972, in *William Henry Hastie: The High Mountain, A Commemorative Symposium at the Harvard Law School (November 16, 1984)*, 9.

23 Kluger, *Simple Justice*,127.

24 Jack Greenberg, *Crusaders in the Courts* (New York: BasicBooks, A Division of HarperCollins Publishers, Inc.,1994), 20.

25 The NAACP and Houston had disagreed and parted in 1938, but Houston continued to advise the LDF.

In his early years of command at the LDF, Marshall leaned heavily on his former professors. Hastie and Marshall argued two cases before the Supreme Court: *Smith v. Allwright*, 321 U.S. 649 (1944), which established the right to vote for blacks in Democratic Party primaries in the South (where the Democratic primary was the effective election), and *Irene Morgan v. Commonwealth of Virginia*, 328 U.S. 373 (1946), which outlawed segregated interstate motor travel.

At oral argument in *Morgan*, Hastie was questioned by Justice Wiley Rutledge (for whom Pollak would clerk in two years). Pollak relates that Justice Rutledge proposed to Hastie that perhaps the real question at hand was not the commerce clause (on which the case was argued) but equal protection under the Fourteenth Amendment—that is, the constitutionality of segregation. Hastie responded that he was not addressing that point, but would bring it before the Court in a subsequent case.[26]

Hastie felt that they were not yet ready to take on *Plessy* and the Fourteenth Amendment. The subsequent case he forecasted would take six more years to appear; the strategy for *Brown v. Board of Education* was, at this time, still evolving.

1950

In 1950 LDF had reached a turning point. First, there was the passing of the old guard. Charles Hamilton Houston died in April, and Hastie gave the eulogy: "He guided us through the legal wilderness of second-class citizenship. He was truly the Moses of that journey. He lived to see us close to the promised land of full equality under the law, closer than even he dared hope when he set out on that journey and so much closer than would have been possible without his genius and his leadership" (26 April 1950).[27]

At the time of Houston's death, Hastie had already been appointed to the Third Circuit Court of Appeals by President Truman in a recess appointment in October 1949, although his nomination would not reach the Senate floor until July 1950. This meant that Judge Hastie could not participate in the further preparation of any lawsuits. Finally, on 19 July 1950, William H. Hastie became the first black attorney confirmed by the U.S. Senate to a U.S. appellate court—the U.S. Appellate Court for the Third Circuit. This left Thurgood Marshall with the full responsibility for the direction and operation of the LDF.

It was into this arena that Pollak, invited by Coleman, stepped in early 1950. Aware of his minority status as a white, Pollak remembered

26 Louis H. Pollak, discussion with Leanna Lee Whitman, September 2010.

27 William H. Hastie, "Charles H. Houston (1895–1950)," *The Crisis*, 365 (June 1950).

feeling more at ease after Thurgood Marshall introduced him to Walter White, secretary (head) of the NAACP and LDF. During one strategy meeting, White came to call on "his lawyers"; Marshall was very diplomatic and began introducing those present, who had formed themselves into a line. Pollak recalls standing at the end of the line. In turn Thurgood graciously introduced him: "This is Louis Pollak. I think you know his father." White: "Yes, indeed. I worked with your pappy in the Scottsboro cases." Pollak felt that White had given him his blessing. He watched as White and Marshall went off, and an image of two Southern gentlemen sitting on a porch drinking mint juleps came to mind.[28]

Jack Greenberg, whom Thurgood Marshall had hired in 1949, was a fresh, brilliant graduate out of Columbia Law School, and, like Pollak, white and Jewish. Jack observed:

> There was no question that he [Pollak] would employ his considerable talents at something other than getting rich. Tall, thin, ascetic looking, but rarely without a smile, he came to civil rights not only by conviction, but by descent and marriage.
>
> One day as we worked together on an early phase of the school cases, Lou and I met at the Columbia law library and took a walk outside and speculated about how we hoped to spend our careers. We agreed that we would be happy if we could work at matters we cared about so long as we could earn five or six thousand dollars a year.[29]

Pollak saw Thurgood Marshall chiefly in group lawyer sessions at which Pollak was a very junior participant. He found that some of these sessions were impossibly large, with thirty or forty there, whereas those that had as few six or eight or ten were correspondingly more workable: "I used to find them very frustrating because they were so undisciplined—often never seemed to get anywhere. Too much time was taken out for jokes, storytelling, diversion—30 minutes or maybe an hour at a time, interrupting the substantive flow."[30]

In retrospect Pollak realized that there was probably no other way strategy meetings could have been orchestrated, given the dynamics of the people involved. And the meetings could be great fun: "Thurgood was the ringmaster. We were always shouting at one another. Some would pound the table. Finally Thurgood would say, 'Okay. I've heard

28 Louis H. Pollak, interview with Leanna Lee Whitman, 1 November 2011.

29 Greenberg, *Crusaders in the Court*, 160. Lou Pollak, however, remembered the agreed-to sum as ten thousand dollars a year. Louis H. Pollak, interview with Leanna Lee Whitman, 1 November 2011.

30 Louis H. Pollak, interview with Richard Kluger, 25 June 1971, Brown vs. Board of Education Collection (MS759), Series 1, Box 4, Folder 80, Manuscripts and Archives, Yale University Library.

enough. This is the way we're going to do it.' Then everybody would climb back on their stools until the next argument."[31]

Pollak viewed Marshall as a commanding leader in charge of many contending interests around the country:

> Thurgood could operate across the nation with all his skills, but when he went anywhere to try a case or represent somebody, he was always poaching on someone else's territory—and that someone may not have been as educated or sophisticated or as talented but he was a local potentate nonetheless—and he had to be honored as such.
>
> The NAACP was a huge network of people, and the Inc. Fund had hundreds of clients and the whole enterprise couldn't be run monolithically but had to coalesce, had to get its spirit out of a sense of felt need arising in the communities of people willing to take the time and the risks to fight for what they wanted. Thus, Thurgood had a very complex job of diplomacy to make the whole operation coherent, well-timed, and executed with a keen sense of where the courts were. These group meetings of lawyers were aimed at achieving a kind of political consensus and to make clear that the Inc. Fund's movements were not merely an extension of Thurgood's own desires and personality.[32]

Pollak observed that Marshall's key advisers were Robert Ming, Jr., Spottswood W. Robinson III, and, very rapidly, William Coleman, Jr. Bob Ming taught at the University of Chicago, the first black professor appointed to the faculty of a major white law school. Spot Robinson was a Howard Law School graduate and student of Houston and Hastie. He later became dean of Howard Law School and was subsequently appointed to the U.S. Court of Appeals for the District of Columbia Circuit.

> My impression was that Bob Ming was the most commanding fellow after Thurgood—Ming was a forceful, eloquent talker, a helluva good lawyer, though ultimately his instinct for strategy was not a match for Thurgood, but he was surely Thurgood's equal on the doctrinal level. . . . At the other extreme in manner, possessing the quietest, tiniest voice—but a voice that was listened to—was Spot Robinson. If Spot disagreed, Thurgood thought there was something there to worry about . . . Ming might say, "They *got* to listen to us," and Spot might come back simply, "No, they *don't* got to listen." . . . Another important voice was Bill Coleman. His relationship with Thurgood was special; Marshall recognized a range of experience, a quality of intellect unique in so young a man.[33]

31 Louis H. Pollak, discussion with Leanna Lee Whitman, September 2010.

32 Louis H. Pollak, interview with Richard Kluger, 25 June 1971.

33 Id.

Pollak said Marshall was always deferential to James Nabrit, Jr., who after graduating at the top of his class and as an editor of the law review at Northwestern Law School, became a successful partner in a black firm in Houston. He later served as dean of Howard Law School, president of Howard University, and ambassador to the United Nations.[34]

Pollak recalled that Robert Carter was a good number two man—he complemented Marshall by assuming a managerial role set within the framework that Thurgood set down: "[Carter was] very effective within his category, but less good at creative aspects. . . ."[35]

One example of how Marshall dealt with internal controversy can be seen in his handling of the "doll man." Kenneth Clark and his wife, Mamie Phipps Clark, were social psychologists whose research focused on the psychological effects of segregation on black children. Chief among the Clarks' tests was the doll test. Using dolls that differed in color only, one brown and one white, the psychologists asked children to choose: give me the doll that you like the best; give me the nice doll; give me the doll that looks bad; give me the doll with the nice color. The Clarks found that a vast majority of black children from an early age showed an unmistakable preference for the white doll. The Clarks thus viewed the tests not as making a precise statement on school segregation, but rather as describing the effect of social discrimination, of which school segregation was a part.[36]

Within Thurgood's team, the question whether to use Clark's evidence in the school cases briefs stirred strong sentiments and division. Robert Carter was a steadfast advocate for inclusion; Lou Pollak was skeptical; Bob Ming and Bill Coleman strongly against. Coleman wanted to make a purely legal case. "From my clerkship days I imagined with horror how the skeptical justices might derisively view evidence based on children's dolls."[37] Thurgood heard everyone out. Finally, he made the decision to go with the Clark research because he viewed the evidence as directly on point, contradicting *Plessy's* claim that segregation does not imply racial inferiority. Coleman erupted, "Jesus Christ, those damn dolls! I thought it was a joke."[38]

---

34 Louis H. Pollak, interview with Leanna Lee Whitman, 1 November 2011.

35 Louis H. Pollak, interview with Richard Kluger, 25 June 1971.

36 Greenberg, *Crusaders in the Court*, 124.

37 Coleman, *Counsel for the Situation*, 123.

38 Id. at 123. Chief Justice Earl Warren in the *Brown v. Board of Education* decision in footnote 11 summarized the social science evidence showing the detrimental effects of segregation on black school children. Footnote 11 has proven to be extremely controversial, sparking criticism that the Supreme Court decision in *Brown* was based on social science, not legal reasoning.

Marshall's Attack on Segregation

Thurgood Marshall, following Houston's strategy, led the LDF battle against segregation by attacking graduate schools in the South first. The U.S. Supreme Court in *Sipuel v. Board of Regents of the University of Oklahoma* (1948)[39] required the university to provide Ada Sipuel, an African American to whom it had denied admission to a state law school, with an equal legal education.

A few years later when the University of Oklahoma admitted George McLaurin to its all-white graduate study in education, it made McLaurin sit in the hall outside the classroom and at a separate table in the library and dining hall because state law required that graduate studies be on "a segregated basis." For a unanimous Court, Chief Justice Fred Vinson held in *McLaurin v. Oklahoma State Regents* (1950)[40] that the university's treatment violated the Equal Protection Clause of the Fourteenth Amendment. The Court held that "the Fourteenth Amendment precludes differences in treatment by the state based upon race."[41]

McLaurin was a companion case to *Sweatt v. Painter*.[42] In this case, Sweatt was denied admission to the state-supported University of Texas Law School solely because he was African American, since Texas law forbade the admission of African Americans to the state law school. Sweatt was offered, but refused, enrollment in a separate law school newly established for African Americans by the state. Again, writing for a unanimous Court, Chief Justice Fred Vinson concluded that there was no objective way that a newly created state law school for African Americans could be equal to the University of Texas Law School.

Widening the Wedge

McLaurin was argued on 3–4 April, and *Sweatt* on 4 April 1950. The U.S. Supreme Court decided both cases with unanimous decisions on 5 June 1950. Houston's strategy of tightly focused attacks on professional and graduate schools had led to some unambiguous victories in the Supreme Court. But going forward, the question now became choosing the degree to which LDF needed to widen its scope to reach the goal of racial integration. Their choices were: 1) attack at the college level where attendance was voluntary; 2) attack at the public high school and elementary school levels where attendance was

39 *Sipuel v. Board of Regents of the University of Oklahoma*, 332 U.S. 631 (1948).

40 *McLaurin v. Oklahoma State Regents for Higher Education*, 339 U.S. 637 (1950).

41 Id. at 642.

42 *Sweatt v. Painter*, 339 U.S. 629 (1950).

generally compulsory; or 3) mount a frontal attack on *Plessy*—charge that segregation by race on any level of education was unconstitutional.

After much consideration of deeply held, but often conflicting, advice, Marshall decided to move from Houston's narrow wedge to Margold's original plan. He would broaden the fight against segregation by moving down to high schools and elementary schools. Strategically, the NAACP Legal Defense Fund would file suit in as many venues as it could, charging that at the very least, school facilities were inferior and therefore unconstitutional (following *McLaurin* and *Sweatt*). But the LDF would also take on *Plessy* and charge that segregation by race in schools, by itself, was unconstitutional.

Pollak had been wary of the school strategy: "If it had been my responsibility to decide how to proceed in the wake of *Sipuel, Sweatt* etc., I think I would not have had the courage to go after segregation *per se* and at the school level. I would first have tried to erode the doctrine of separate but equal at places where attendance was not compulsory. . . ."[43]

In the end, however, Pollak felt that "Thurgood's strategy was daring and successful. His role [was that of an] absolutely unique kind of broker. In his leadership function he was master of making all participants feel important, but within the orbit of Thurgood himself, he made the decisions. Yes, he had the ability to clown, to be raconteur, an endlessly good listener, flattering to his chronological seniors yet keeping intellectual control of the whole enterprise."[44]

Having made the decision to attack *Plessy* head-on as part of his strategy, Marshall and the LDF went to the 1950 NAACP convention in Boston and got it approved.[45]

The School Cases

In the next year, from late 1950 to 1951, LDF lawyers unveiled their strategy. They used the tactic of filing in federal three-judge district courts, which they had first used successfully in *Sipuel*, 1948. A constitutional allegation established jurisdiction in a federal three-judge district court, which at the time provided a direct right of appeal to the U.S. Supreme Court.[46] The advantage of the three-judge court

43 Louis H. Pollak, interview with Richard Kluger, 25 June 1971.

44 Ibid.

45 Greenberg, *Crusaders in the Court*, 85.

46 A federal three-judge district court is a panel of three federal judges convened to hear a trial in which a statute is challenged on constitutional grounds. Established in 1913, federal three-judge district courts were widely used during the Civil Rights era but were severly curtailed in 1976, when Congress restricted their jurisdiction to constitutional challenges to congressional reapportionments. For a concise review and analysis of the evolution of the

over the usual appellate process was that the U.S. Supreme Court was highly selective in taking appeals that came from the federal circuit courts, and a case wending its way through the ordinary federal appellate labyrinth could move at a glacial speed.

Accordingly, LDF lawyers sought cases in which there were already existing conflicts in segregated public school systems. Working with local counsel, they filed complaints in federal three-judge district courts alleging the inequality of separate facilities and the unconstitutionality of the state statute or the state constitution involving public school segregation in Kansas, South Carolina, Virginia, and Delaware.

Independent of the LDF school cases, James Nabrit, Jr. filed a complaint in a United States District Court alleging the unconstitutionality of segregated District of Columbia public schools.[47] After losing in the district court, Nabrit prepared for a hearing before the United States Court of Appeals.[48]

Reaction to the new turn in LDF strategy—branching out to elementary and high schools and directly taking on *Plessy*—was vigorous and often negative. Marjorie McKenzie, a black lawyer and columnist for the *Pittsburgh Courier*, was a vociferous critic who spoke for those concerned that a major setback could put them back years: "Since the inroads made on segregation by the NAACP's own victories of June 1950 in the *Sweatt* and *McLaurin* cases . . . the NAACP has filed 'pure' segregation test cases. . . . Though these are logical extensions, in theory, of the segregation cases of last June, they involve risk where none was necessary. . . ."[49]

Thurgood Marshal rebutted:

> The column points out that the *Sweatt* and *McLaurin* decisions did not destroy *Plessy v. Ferguson*. This is technically true. On the other hand, a reading of these decisions will reveal that although it did not destroy the doctrine as such, it took away from the doctrine the implication that it could never be attacked. . . .
>
> . . . [I]nsofar as elementary and high schools are concerned, the South made no effort to equalize facilities until we started these elementary and high school cases. Now they are rushing with everything they have to try to bring about what they call equality. It is completely unrealistic to believe that the South will voluntarily, of its own free will, without affirmative action on our part, equalize school

three-judge district courts and their significance during the Civil Rights era, see Michael E. Solimine, *Congress, Ex Parte Young, and the Three-Judge District Court*, 70 U.Pitt. L. Rev. 101, 125–134 (2008).

47 *Spottswood Thomas Bolling, et al. v. C. Melvin Sharpe, et al.* (Washington, D.C.).

48 Kluger, *Simple Justice*, 523.

49 Marjorie McKenzie, *Pursuit of Democracy: McKenzie in Challenge on Legal* Tactics, Courier (7 July 1951).

> facilities or any other governmental facilities. If we had not threatened to challenge the legality of the segregation system and if we do not continue the challenge to segregated schools we will get the same thing we have been getting all these years—separate but never equal.[50]

Not surprisingly, the LDF lost its cases in Kansas, South Carolina, and Virginia, which they promptly appealed to the U.S. Supreme Court. Delaware, on the other hand, proved different.

Jack Greenberg and legendary black lawyer (Delaware's only black lawyer at the time) Louis Redding filed their Delaware school cases in federal court, anticipating going before a federal three-judge district court. However, the state moved under the doctrine of abstention that the federal court do nothing until the state court first had an opportunity to construe the segregation statute.[51] So Greenberg and Redding had to go to state court, but their objections were mollified because an exceptional chancellor (judge), Collins J. Seitz, presided.

Jack Greenberg and Louis Redding had first appeared before Vice-Chancellor Seitz in 1950 when the NAACP brought suit against the University of Delaware for refusing to admit black students. Greenberg knew that Seitz "would have to think twice about whether he would be reelected [by the Delaware Legislature], promoted, or forced to return to private practice before ruling in our favor."[52] Yet during the trial, "he [Seitz] drove to both the University of Delaware (white) and Delaware State College (black) at breakneck speed, our [Greenberg's and Redding's] car in pursuit, to inspect them."[53] Seitz ruled in *Parker v. University of Delaware*[54] that the University of Delaware did not meet the standard of "separate but equal" under *Plessy*. He ordered the university to admit blacks. The ruling marked the first time a state public university was desegregated by court order anywhere in the nation.

Notwithstanding his decision in *Parker,* Seitz was appointed chancellor of the Court of Chancery in 1951. Redding recalls that "the University of Delaware case had made Seitz a lot of enemies, and we didn't want him to have this much additional heat on him by having to decide the school cases as well."[55] But Greenberg and Redding went before Chancellor Seitz with two other school desegregation cases:

---

50 Thurgood Marshall, Courier (14 July 1951).

51 Greenberg, *Crusaders in the Courts*, 136.

52 Id. at 88.

53 Id. at 88.

54 *Parker v. Univ. of Delaware*, 31 Del. Ch. 381, 75 A.2d 225 (1950).

55 Kluger, *Simple Justice*, 436.

Belton v. Gebhart and *Bulah v. Gebhart.*[56] In *Belton* black students sought admission at a geographically closer white high school that offered many classes and extracurricular activities not available at the black high school they were forced to attend. Similarly, in *Bulah* a black elementary school student was not allowed to take the bus that stopped by her home or attend the geographically closer white elementary school. (The cases were heard together because of the similarities they presented.)

Before issuing his ruling in *Belton/Bulah*, Seitz decided again to see for himself the differences between the black and white elementary and high schools. He concluded that state-imposed segregation in education itself caused black children, as a class, to receive substantially inferior educational opportunities.[57] Seitz ruled that segregation was unconstitutional because it violated the equal protection clause of the Constitution, and he "ordered the immediate admission of black students to the white schools shown to be superior." To do otherwise, he explained, "is to say to a plaintiff: Yes, your Constitutional rights are being invaded, but be patient, we will see whether in time they are still violated."[58] Furthermore, he issued a call to the Supreme Court to strike down *Plessy*. The "separate but equal doctrine in education should be rejected, but . . . its rejection must come from [the Supreme] Court."[59] Five months later the Delaware Supreme Court upheld Seitz's opinion. Therefore—as Pollak was always careful to point out—in the school cases included in *Brown, Belton/Bulah* was the only case tried in state court and the only case in which the court ordered immediate desegregation.

The state of Delaware (like the other states faced with school desegregation cases) had argued that even if segregated public schools were found unequal, the state should be given time "to bring the separate schools up to par." But Seitz did not accept this argument because he believed that black schools would never receive funding equal to that of white schools.[60]

---

56 *Gebhart v. Belton*; *Bulah v. Gebhart,* 87 A.2d 862 (1952).

57 Id. at 865.

58 Id. at 870.

59 Id. at 865.

60 The Honorable Collins Jacques Seitz, "Cases Recalled," interviewed by David V. Stivison, 14 July 1993, William H. Hastie Library, United States Court of Appeals for the Third Circuit. Seitz was appointed to the Third Circuit Court of Appeals in 1966, and was serving as chief judge of the appellate court (1971–84) when Pollak was appointed to the district court, Eastern District of Pennsylvania in 1978. Although the two became acquainted and Pollak greatly respected Seitz, Judge Pollak and Chief Judge Seitz regrettably never spoke about their shared experiences in *Brown.*

Brown v. Board of Education Goes to the Supreme Court

The U.S. Supreme Court bundled all of the LDF state cases and the Washington, D.C. case under what is known as *Brown v. Board of Education:* 1) *Oliver Brown, et al. v. Board of Education of Topeka, Shawnee County, Kansas, et al.*; 2) *Harry Briggs, Jr. et al. v. Elliott, et al.* (South Carolina); 3) *Dorothy Davis, et al. v. County School Board Prince Edward County, Virginia, et al.*; 4) *Spottswood Thomas Bolling, et al. v. C. Melvin Sharpe, et al.* (District of Columbia); 5) *Francis B. Gebhart, et al. v. Ethel Louise Belton, et al.* (Delaware).[61]

Pollak continued working with the LDF *Brown* team after leaving Paul, Weiss in 1951 to accept a position as attorney/special assistant to Ambassador-at-large Philip C. Jessup in the Department of State. As *Brown* got closer to the Supreme Court, it was evident that Pollak's status as a young LDF volunteer looking in from the periphery had evolved into that of a trusted and valued adviser. Jack Greenberg recalled that Pollak "wrote briefs, made arguments, gave advice hundreds and hundreds of times on issues of the highest level of constitutional sophistication. Innumerable LDF briefs presented concepts that he formulated. . . . He helped me—and others—prepare many an argument of our own and words mouthed by some of us sometimes really were his."[62] Bill Coleman's version of Pollak's contribution to *Brown*: "I think we [Pollak and Coleman] have an understanding—if he dies first, I can say that I wrote most of the [*Brown*] brief. If I die first, he can say he wrote it."[63]

The NAACP Legal Defense Fund filed an appellant brief with the Supreme Court on 23 September 1952. In thirteen pages, the appellants presented two arguments. First, a statute that permits classification of public school students on the basis of race and color alone violates the equal protection clause of the Fourteenth Amendment. Second, the district court's finding that segregation adversely affects the segregated child's ability to learn was a finding of inequality that posed a violation of equal protection.

---

61 How the Supreme Court came to list *Brown* first is unclear and open to speculation.

62 Jack Greenberg, "Louis H. Pollak," *127 U.Pa.L.Rev.* 283, 295 (1978–79). Kathy Pollak recalled that Thurgood Marshall called their home frequently and at all hours seeking Lou Pollak's advice on LDF cases.

Katherine Weiss Pollak, discussion with Leanna Lee Whitman, 14 August 2012.

Pollak's name does not appear on the 1952 *Brown* brief. Former Supreme Court clerks were prohibited from appearing before the Court for three years after their clerkship ended, and Pollak ended his internship with Justice Wiley Rutledge in 1949.

63 William T. Coleman, 21 May 2010, Special Session of the Court "Portrait Presentation of the Hon. U.S. District Court Louis H. Pollak."

Then the NAACP lawyers waited for a reply to their brief from Kansas. Similar briefs had been filed against Virginia and South Carolina and answers to those briefs were duly received. But no answer came from Kansas. According to Pollak, LDF members kept asking each other, "Where is Kansas? Where is it?"[64]

Representing Kansas in *Brown v. Board of Education*

In the Kansas state attorney general's office, Paul Wilson, new assistant attorney general, often asked the same question. Wilson had joined the Kansas attorney general's office in December 1951 in part to get appellate court experience. Shortly after his arrival, the attorney general handed over the *Brown v. Board of Education* file to Wilson, and instructed him to help write the first draft of a brief in support of the state's position. The attorney general emphasized that he did not intend to support the segregation policy of the Topeka Board of Education, but would argue only that the Kansas statute was constitutional because *Plessy v. Ferguson* (separate but equal) and *Gong Lum v. Rice* (all-white public schools were constitutional) remained the law of the land.[65]

However, despite the impending appeal of *Brown* before the Supreme Court, neither the Kansas governor's office nor the Kansas attorney general's office gave any further orders. In fact, Wilson in late November "had become reconciled to a future without *Brown*, without a trip to Washington at taxpayer expense, and without admission to the Supreme Court bar."[66]

The inaction of the state of Kansas did not go unnoticed. On 24 November 1952, the U.S. Supreme Court issued an order directed to the Kansas attorney general: "Because of the national importance of the issue presented and because of its importance to the State of Kansas, we request that the State present its views at oral argument."[67] Like it or not, Kansas was a player in *Brown*. When the attorney general returned to his office on 28 November, he discussed the appeal with Wilson. Instructing Wilson to file in defense of the constitutionality of the Kansas statute, the attorney general handed him the *Brown* file and said, "Take the damned thing and do your best."[68] And so Wilson, who

---

64 Louis H. Pollak, interview with Leanna Lee Whitman, October 2010.

65 Paul E. Wilson, *A Time to Lose: Representing Kansas in Brown v. Board of Education* (Lawrence, Kansas: University Press of Kansas, 1995), 71. Louis H. Pollak directed me to this source: "You always need to hear out the other side. And it's a good read."

66 Id. at 117.

67 *Brown et al. v. Board of Education et al.*, 344 U.S. 141 (1952).

68 Wilson, *A Time to Lose*, 120.

personally did not believe in segregation,[69] found himself on 4 December 1952 on a train headed for his first visit to Washington, D.C. He was scheduled to argue his first appellate case, which would be before the U.S. Supreme Court on 9 December; Wilson had with him fifty copies of the Kansas brief along with his new $45.00 blue suit.[70]

Oral Argument before the Supreme Court: 9 December 1952

Arguments in the School Segregation Cases[71] began at 1:35 p.m., 9 December. The nine justices sitting were Chief Justice Fred Vinson and Justices Hugo Black, Stanley Reed, Felix Frankfurter, William Douglas, Robert Jackson, Harold Burton, Tom Clark, and Sherman Minton.[72]

Bob Carter led off for the LDF in Kansas "in a style typical of mainstream appellate argument—conversational, not terribly loud, not very aggressive, perhaps even a little softer than ordinary. He did not leave any doubt that we were going all the way: 'Here we abandon any claim, in pressing our attack on the unconstitutionality of this statute—we abandon any claim—any constitutional inequality which comes from anything other than the act of segregation itself.'"[73]

Following Wilson for Kansas, Thurgood Marshall was up next to argue *Briggs v. Elliott* (South Carolina). Jack Greenberg noted that "Thurgood spoke slowly, for him, on this occasion, making sure to articulate his words in an educated Southern way, rather than in the country style he often used."[74] Just before he sat down, Justice Jackson asked Thurgood whether his arguments would affect American Indians and Thurgood responded, "I think that it would. But I think that the biggest trouble with the Indians is that they have not had the judgment or the wherewithal to bring lawsuits." Justice Jackson: "Maybe you should bring some up." Marshall: "I have a full load now, Mr. Justice."[75]

69 Id. at 7.

70 Id. at 126.

71 The U.S. Supreme Court grouped *Bolling* with the LDF school cases under *Brown v. Board of Education* for the oral arguments. But the Court issued separate decisions for the states under *Brown* because it focused on Fourteenth Amendment equal protection and for *Bolling* because it focused on Fifth Amendment due process.

72 Louis Pollak was working for the State Department at the time of the 1952 *Brown* oral argument and consequently decided not to attend. Louis H. Pollak, interview with Leanna Lee Whitman, October 2010.

73 Greenberg, *Crusaders in the Courts*, 169.

74 Id. at 168.

75 Friedman, *Brown v. Board*, 50–1.

Greenberg noted that the colloquy was important because, in its casual good-naturedness, it showed a kind of rapport and confidence. "Thurgood later told me [Greenberg] that during the argument he flashed the Masonic secret distress signal to Jackson, who signaled back."[76]

The justices, in particular Justice Frankfurter, peppered the counsels with questions. However, when the legendary John W. Davis, in nearly his 140th appearance before the Supreme Court, rose to reply for South Carolina, the justices allowed him to argue almost without interruption.

Following South Carolina were Virginia, Washington, D.C., and finally Delaware. In the last of the five school cases heard, the attorney general of Delaware, Albert Young, went first because he had lost in the state courts under Chancellor Seitz and was now the appellant before the Supreme Court. Young argued that the state had every intention of equalizing the black schools involved; he said Seitz had been wrong in ordering immediate integration rather than equalization because he misunderstood the governing law. Justice Frankfurter responded, "If I may say so, a chancellor who shows as much competence as this opinion shows, probably can read the opinions of this Court with understanding."[77]

At the end of the last session, Bill Coleman reflected that questions from the bench revealed both skepticism and divisiveness indicative of deteriorating relationships among the justices in the Vinson Court.[78] John W. Davis, counsel for South Carolina, on the other hand, interpreted the questions as suggesting a win for the segregated school districts. As he walked out of the Supreme Court building, he was overheard saying to a colleague that based on the comments and questions of the justices, he was likely to win by five to four or perhaps six to three.[79]

However, no such decision came to pass. Instead, on 8 June 1953, as the term came to close, the Court issued an order scheduling all five cases for reargument on 12 October 1953. Insofar as they were relevant to their respective cases, the court order directed the parties to discuss questions about the Fourteenth Amendment's legislative history—whether the Congress that drafted or the state legislatures that ratified the Fourteenth Amendment contemplated or did not contemplate, understood or did not understand, that the amendment would abolish segregation in public schools.

---

76 Greenberg, *Crusaders in the Court*, 170.

77 Friedman, *Brown v. Board*, 159.

78 Coleman, *Counsel for the Situation*, 143.

79 Kluger, *Simple Justice*, 581.

Immediately, the NAACP sent out telegrams asking potential donors for money and seeking research aid from lawyers and legal scholars. Bill Coleman, then a lawyer in a Philadelphia firm, volunteered to coordinate the research efforts of his vast network of contacts, as the Marshall team toiled during the summer. Pollak's 1 August 1953 cover letter to Bob Carter reflects the problematic research results that were beginning to flow into the Marshall team:

> Dear Bob—
> I'm enclosing a copy of a memo Bill suggested I write . . . What little work I've done on the attached memo confirms the proposition that we've got a tough job proving that the equal protection clause was supposed to require integrated education. I'm afraid it can't be done. If we win, it'll be on the basis that the clause requires an increasingly high standard of achievement as times and mores change.
>
> Another line of emphasis, suggested to me a couple of days ago, is that segregated education only became "discriminatory" considerably after the enactment of the Amendment—that the idea of educating Negroes at all was itself a largely novel one in the '60s, etc. This is sort of another way of phrasing the changing standard argument.[80]

Outside events then took a dramatic turn. In September 1953, Chief Justice Vinson unexpectedly died of a heart attack, and President Eisenhower made a recess appointment of California governor Earl Warren to be chief justice of the U.S. Supreme Court. Because Warren's Senate confirmation was delayed, reargument was postponed from 12 October until 7 December 1953. (Warren was confirmed by the U.S. Senate on 1 March 1954.) Unsure of the quality of Earl Warren, a popular governor of California and a moderate Republican who as attorney general of California had nevertheless spearheaded the relocation of Japanese Americans in 1942 after the Japanese attack on Pearl Harbor on 7 December 1941, the Marshall team continued its course.

Jack Greenberg recalled that before the LDF brief was finalized, Thurgood sent the summary of argument (synopsis) outside the staff for comment and editing. Greenberg, who like Marshall often reached out to Pollak, noted that Thurgood had always taught that the summary of argument was the most important part of a brief because most justices read it first, and some don't read beyond it.[81]

So in the summer of 1953, a package came for Pollak:

---

80 Louis Pollak to Robert Carter, 1 August 1953. Box IIB140, Folder 7, NAACP Collection, Library of Congress.

81 Greenberg, *Crusaders*, 189.

> . . . I received a draft of the *Brown* brief from Thurgood, who wanted comments back yesterday. On reading it over I concluded that the section of the draft captioned "Summary of Argument" was deficient. This seemed a matter of serious concern because I knew from experience that judges reading a brief tend to look first at the Summary of Argument with the expectation that this will make clear the principal lines of argument on which counsel relies, the detailed elaboration being contained in the balance of the brief. I decided that I would try to compose a draft of the Summary of Argument. I am not a fast writer but on this occasion I filled pages of a yellow pad with unaccustomed speed.
>
> In the typing pool I gave my handwritten draft to a young typist, very recently out of high school. She promised to work on my request right away and completed it in about twenty minutes. I thanked her and she replied: "Oh Mr. Pollak it was one of the most interesting pieces of work that I have ever read. But may I ask you one question?" Gratified by her praise of what I had written, I of course said, "Yes indeed." Then she put her question: "I wasn't quite sure. Is it that you want the little colored children to go to school with the little white children or not to go to school with the little white children?" It was clear that my revision had to be revised. [82]

Greenberg summed up: Pollak thought the LDF summary of argument wasn't clear and didn't argue forcefully enough. "Lou, who writes beautifully and with great precision . . . rewrote the section."[83]

Pollak's revision, Appellant brief, Reargument of *Brown v. Board of Education*:

> SUMMARY OF ARGUMENT
>
> These cases consolidated for argument before this Court present in different factual contexts essentially the same ultimate legal questions.
>
> The substantive question common to all is whether a state can, consistently with the Constitution, exclude children, solely on the ground that they are Negroes, from public schools which otherwise they would be qualified to attend. It is the thesis of this brief, submitted on behalf of the excluded children, that the answer to the question is in the negative: the Fourteenth Amendment prevents states from according differential treatment to American children on the basis of their color or race. . . .

82 Louis H. Pollak, interview with Leanna Lee Whitman, October 2010.

Although he wrote the summary of argument for the reargument, Louis Pollak's name does not appear on the *Brown* brief because he was working for the State Department at the time the brief was filed.

83 Greenberg, *Crusaders*, 189.

> The importance to our American democracy of the substantive question can hardly be overstated. The question is whether a nation founded on the proposition that "all men are created equal" is honoring its commitments to grant "due process of law" and the "equal protection of the laws" to all within its borders when it, or one of its constituent states, confers or denies benefits on the basis of color or race. . . .
>
> Were these ordinary cases, it might be enough to say that the *Plessy* case can be distinguished—that it involved only segregation in transportation. But these are not ordinary cases, and in deference to their importance it seems more fitting to meet the *Plessy* doctrine head-on and to declare that doctrine erroneous.
>
> Candor requires recognition that the plain purpose and effect of segregated education is to perpetuate an inferior status for Negroes which is America's sorry heritage from slavery. But the primary purpose of the Fourteenth Amendment was to deprive the states of *all* power to perpetuate such a caste system.[84]

Three weeks before the 7 December scheduled reargument, Thurgood Marshall and Bill Coleman moved into a suite at the Wardman Park Hotel in Washington. According to Coleman, their separate bedrooms connected to a comfortable living area, which quickly became cluttered with briefs, records, federal reporters, and a bottle or two of Jack Daniel's Tennessee whiskey.[85]

The LDF team, as it did prior to all Supreme Court cases, conducted a moot court at Howard Law School, which was then housed in the basement of the university's Founders' Library. Pollak recalled, "At the dry run at Howard before the '53 reargument, the student or faculty member standing in for Justice Jackson asked a question similar to what he had asked at the original argument: 'What troubles me, Mr. Marshall, is whether this Court has the power to grant the relief you seek in this matter—I ask you, do we have the power?' And Thurgood fell on one knee, Al-Jolson-like, and said, supplicant-like: 'Power? Power? White boss, you got the power to do anything *you* want.'–breaking up the house."[86]

---

84 *Brown v. Board of Education*, 347 U.S. 483 (1954), brief for appellants on reargument, at 15–7.

85 Coleman, *Counsel for the Situation*, 148.

86 Louis H. Pollak, interview with Richard Kluger, 25 June 1971. Kluger, however, states that Marshall did not participate in the dry run before *Brown*, but instead hovered. See Kluger, *Simple Justice*, 562.

Reargument, 7 December 1953

On 7 December 1953, Day of Infamy and Pollak's thirty-first birthday, Bill Coleman and Thurgood Marshall took a cab from the Wardman Park Hotel. The taxi driver, a man of color, quietly drove the pair for twenty-five minutes to the Supreme Court. When they arrived, he spoke up: "Neither of you gentlemen ever told me where you wanted to go. But I knew, Mr. Marshall, where you had to be at 12:00 noon. God bless you sir."[87]

In reargument the consolidated cases of South Carolina and Virginia went first. Spottswood Robinson led off with historical arguments that the purpose of the Fourteenth Amendment was to achieve complete legal equality. Robinson spoke for about forty minutes before Justice Frankfurter asked a question about the weight to be given to individual congressional statements and Justice Reed asked several questions about the power of Congress.

Marshall followed and began to review the basis of Supreme Court decisions in the more recent cases of racial classification laws interpreting the broadening scope of the Fourteenth Amendment. The justices, however, were not interested. Interruptions came in rapid succession beginning with Justice Jackson: "I do not believe the Court was troubled about its own cases. It has done a good deal of reading of those cases."[88] Justice Jackson, along with the other justices, was interested in the power of the judiciary to act in the absence of congressional action on state segregation laws. Clearly taken aback, Marshall reserved his remaining fifteen minutes for rebuttal.

John W. Davis, patrician Southerner, followed Marshall. From all accounts, Davis gave an eloquent, cogent argument with lengthy citations to the historical record that neither Congress nor the states that ratified the Fourteenth Amendment intended it to be used to force integration in public schools. Blunting the reach of the judiciary, he declared, "Your Honors do not sit, and cannot sit as a glorified Board of Education for the State of South Carolina or any other state. Neither can the District Court."[89] Davis concluded: "Here is equal education, not promised, not prophesied, but present. Shall it be thrown away on some fancied question of racial prestige?"[90] After counsel for Virginia presented, Court was adjourned until the next day.

---

87 Coleman, *Counsel for the Situation*, 150.

88 Friedman, *Brown v. Board*, 195.

89 Id. at 216.

90 Id. at 216.

Coleman reported that he and Marshall returned to their suite at the Wardman Park Hotel, where Pollak joined them. Coleman and Pollak gave rapid-fire critiques of each of the arguments presented at Court and suggestions for rebuttal. Coleman remembers that for four hours they vigorously debated, "facilitated by Marshall's old friend, Jack Daniel," the smoke from Marshall's Winston cigarettes stinging their eyes. Marshall seemed to thrive on the freewheeling exchange. But he kept his own counsel.[91]

The next day in his rebuttal, Marshall regained his mastery. In a Southern folksy drawl, he observed, "As Mr. Davis said yesterday, the only thing the Negroes are trying to get is prestige. Exactly correct. Ever since the Emancipation Proclamation, the Negro has been trying to get . . . the same status as anybody else regardless of race."[92]

Pollak summarized:

> And so the Court decided in Thurgood Marshall's way. But the Court didn't phrase it in terms of prestige. The Court phrased it in terms of sustaining a lower court finding that segregation by itself, without regard to the comparative physical facilities of black and white schools, was disparaging to the black children who were segregated, and those disparaging effects were made the more damaging because the segregation, having been imposed by law, denoted the inferiority of black children. That essentially was the grounding of the opinion that Chief Justice Warren issued for the Court—a Court that was unanimous as it had not been unanimous in *Dred Scott* or in *Plessy*.[93]

But Pollak knew that the *Brown* decision in 1954 with its moral clarity was not the end of the struggle. The speed at which desegregation was to take place was yet to be decided. In 1955, after another round of arguments, Chief Justice Warren wrote *Brown II*,[94] a second unanimous decision. But the Supreme Court—unlike Chancellor Seitz, who ordered immediate desegregation of the Delaware public schools in *Belton*—issued an enigmatic "with all deliberate speed" desegregation order. Therefore, in Pollak's eyes *Cooper v. Aaron*[95] in 1958 was equal in importance to *Brown* because it was the first significant test of the enforcement of *Brown*.[96]

---

91 Coleman, *Counsel for the Situation*, 153. Lou Pollak, however, did not remember this session.

Louis H. Pollak, interview with Leanna Lee Whitman, October 2010.

92 Friedman, *Brown v. Board*, 236.

93 Louis H. Pollak, "Moderator's Remarks: Symposium on the Fiftieth Anniversary of *Brown v. Board of Education*," *Proc. Amer. Phil. Soc.* 148.4 (December 2004):431–32.

94 *Brown v. Board of Education*, 349 U.S. 294 (1955).

95 *Cooper v. Aaron*, 358 U.S. 1 (1958). Louis H. Pollak is listed on the *Cooper v. Aaron* Brief for Respondents.

96 Louis H. Pollak, interview with Leanna Lee Whitman, October 2010.

In Little Rock, Arkansas governor Orval Faubus defied the U.S. Supreme Court and President Eisenhower by keeping nine black students from entering Central High School. The Supreme Court met in an emergency session, and in an unprecedented action, all nine justices signed the *Cooper* opinion ordering immediate desegregation and ruling that governors and state legislatures were bound by the decisions of the U.S. Supreme Court.

In short, Pollak saw the 1954 decision in *Brown* as a milestone, which resoundingly affirmed that the United States judicial system protects the constitutional rights of a minority. As he eloquently phrased it: "The Supreme Court had at last brought the nation into compliance with its founding principle, promulgated in the Declaration of Independence and reaffirmed by Abraham Lincoln at Gettysburg, that 'all men are created equal.'"[97] But contrary to frequently expressed opinion that in the United States times had changed so much that *Brown* could not have been lost, Pollak never felt that the *Brown* decision was a slam dunk: "I was not at all sure that *Brown* was going to win as presented to Court, and I have found the assumption that the case couldn't be lost a source of constant irritation in later years."[98]

Thus Pollak, while a faculty member at Yale Law School, continued to work with LDF. In 1962, he flew with Jack Greenberg to Montgomery, Alabama, for the trial of *Abernathy v. State,* a Freedom Ride case in which eleven defendants (four white and seven black) were charged with breach of peace and unlawful assembly. Greenberg recalls that Pollak "put up with the grimy Jim Crow treatment civil rights lawyers endured, and suffered the unpleasantness of Birmingham, Alabama during the great demonstrations led by Martin Luther King. He gave legal advice, but also met with friends . . . in an effort to help secure a settlement."[99] Later, on 12 October 1964, Pollak argued *Abernathy v. Alabama* (380 US 447 [1965]) before the U.S. Supreme Court. In that case he conversationally recreated a visual image of the Montgomery bus station lunch counter scene: "They [the Freedom Riders] entered a rear entrance to the 'white' waiting room. They entered a rear door somewhat behind where Mr. Justice White's seat would be. . . . Inside the waiting room was a lunch counter. . . . If I may use your bench as that lunch counter curved around to about where Mr. [Anthony] Lewis is sitting. . . . And back over there, somewhat to the rear of Mr. Justice Brennan was a ticket counter."[100] The U.S. Supreme Court reversed the Alabama court convictions without opinion.

---

97 Louis H. Pollak in Cook, *Justice*, 46.

98 Louis H. Pollak, interview with Richard Kluger, 25 June 1971.

99 Jack Greenberg, "Louis H. Pollak," *127 U.Pa.L.Rev.* 283, 296 (1978–79).

100 Louis H. Pollak, "Appellant Oral Argument," 12 October 1964, *Abernathy v.*

With Bill Coleman on 13–14 October 1964, Pollak argued *McLaughlin v. Florida* (379 US 184 [1964]), in which the U.S. Supreme Court held that the Florida law prohibiting an unmarried—black and white—couple from living together denied the equal protection of laws guaranteed by the Fourteenth Amendment and was therefore unconstitutional.[101]

While he fully recognized the "magnolia" pace of desegregation, ten years after the Supreme Court's decision in *Brown v. Board of Education*, Pollak reiterated his faith that the Court did all that it could do in fostering racial equality:

> The Court has few tools at its disposal. And, generally speaking, it can and should shape only the issues which come before it. Nevertheless, the Court has wide discretion as to what issues to consider and in what sequence. And the only responsible way to exercise that discretion—as Justices bred to the common law know full well—is to relate decisions backward to what has been, forward to what will be, and laterally to the initiatives and capabilities of others who share the job of governing. Looking at the Court's work in the ten years which have elapsed since the *School Segregation Cases* were decided, I think a pattern of highly responsible adjudication emerges.[102]

Regarding the historical significance of *Brown* and the enforcement cases that followed, Pollak wrote that "the judgment in the segregation cases will as the decades pass give ever deeper meaning to our national life. It will endure as long as our Constitution and our democratic faith endure."[103]

Pollak took the desegregation of public schools to heart. While he was a faculty member and dean at Yale Law, he and his wife, Kathy, sent their school-age children to public schools in New Haven, Connecticut. Pollak also served on the New Haven School Board for two years (1963–65), "steering the school system away from the constitutional shoals of school prayer and playing a role in shrinking the de

---

Alabama, 380 US 447 (1965), 7″ audio, 28 min., Special Media Archives and Services Division (NWCS), National Archives and Records Administration.

101 Louis H. Pollak argued two other cases before the U.S. Supreme Court: *United Jewish Organizations of Williamsburgh, Inc. v. Casey*, 430 U.S. 144 (argued 6 Oct. 1976, decided 1 Mar. 1977), in which the Supreme Court held constitutional a New York State voting reapportionment plan that was based on a fixed racial quota to correct discrimination against non-whites; and *Rogers v. Richmond*, 365 U.S. 534 (argued 8 and 9 Nov. 1960, decided 20 Mar. 1961), in which the Court ordered a retrial in the lower court because the admissibility of the petitioner's confession was not determined in accordance with standards satisfying the due process clause of the Fourteenth Amendment.

102 Louis H. Pollak, "Ten Years After The Decision," *24 Federal Bar Journal*, 123,131 (Winter 1964).

103 Id. at 132.

facto (not de jure) segregation of our elementary and middle schools by reconfiguring school catchment areas."[104] When asked by a reporter from the *New Haven Register* whether his stances on the New Haven School Board made him a natural for a mayoral candidacy, Pollak deadpanned, "I am the man who took prayer out of public schools and put blacks in. . . ."[105]

And so—with his passion for constitutional rights—it followed that at its 1978 Annual Judicial Conference in the U.S. Virgin Islands, the Third Circuit Court of Appeals (with jurisdiction in Pennsylvania, New Jersey, Delaware, and the U.S. Virgin Islands) asked newly appointed Judge Louis H. Pollak to give a tribute to Judge William H. Hastie (1904–1976), who (besides serving as dean of Howard Law School and NAACP/LDF counsel) had once served as a district court judge and as governor of the U.S. Virgin Islands.

> I ask you to celebrate with me not the brilliant and demanding teacher of law, nor the lawyer who was master of trial and appellate courtrooms, nor the principled and dedicated public official, but the great judge. . . . As his opinions demonstrate, Hastie was a judge of great intellectual power, rare sensitivity, and a long view of the law and its unfolding. But there was more. There was a demeanor. There was a sense of judicial role which put him in place with the Hands and with Cardozo. Which is to say that, once a judge, Hastie knew no client but the law. His duty: to interpret the law without fear or favor . . . and to protect and defend legal institutions and the legal process.[106]

---

104 Louis H. Pollak in Cook, *Justice*, 46.

105 Katherine Weiss Pollak, discussion with Leanna Lee Whitman, 17 August 2012. Kathy Pollak believes that on Lou Pollak's mind at the time was the recent U.S. Supreme Court decision in *Abington School District v. Schempp*, 374 U.S. 203 (1963). In *Schempp*, the Court prohibited the practice of beginning a school day with a prayer or devotional Bible reading in accordance with the First Amendment in its establishment clause (separation of church and state) and applied to the states through the Fourteenth Amendment in its due process clause.

When he was appointed to the New Haven School Board by progressive mayor Dick Lee in 1963, Mayor Lee swore Pollak in at City Hall in an elaborately decorated room with ceremonial flags, with Kathy Pollak and their two oldest daughters, aged eight and ten, attending. Mayor Lee brought out a large Bible and began the ceremony with Pollak repeating the oath until they came to this part:

MAYOR: So help me God.

POLLAK: [*Silence.*]

MAYOR: So help me God.

POLLAK: [*Silence.*]

MAYOR: Oh my God, you're one of those.

Aware that his daughters had retreated behind the ceremonial flags in embarrassment and humiliation at their father's behavior, in the car ride home, Pollak gave them their first lesson on the meaning and significance of the First Amendment.

106 Quoted in Bernard G. Segal, "Louis Pollak," *127 U.Pa.L.Rev.* 283, 310 (1978–79).

Bernard Segal believed that Pollak's masterful portrayal of Judge Hastie was an apt forecast of Louis Pollak on the bench.[107]

And finally in 1992 when the Third Circuit formally opened its new Philadelphia headquarters library, District Court Judge Louis H. Pollak lobbied for the library to be named the William H. Hastie Library. Pollak personally chose the Hastie quotes that were engraved in the library's glass entry panel. And when the Third Circuit Librarian asked Pollak to donate one of his publications to the Court Library's collection, the judge selected *The Constitution and the Supreme Court*[108] and added this inscription:

> I count it a privilege to give these two volumes to the William H. Hastie Library. It is my hope that the reader will find in the volumes a documentary record of the work of the Supreme Court that is consonant with Judge Hastie's enduring views of the Constitution and the judicial process.
>
> May 21, 1993   Louis H. Pollak

Included in Pollak's published collection of Supreme Court cases that are consonant with "Judge Hastie's enduring views of the Constitution and the judicial process" is *Brown v. Board of Education*. *Brown* is also consonant with what Justice David Souter has said set Louis H. Pollak apart—Lou's "moral integrity" and "powerful heart."[109]

---

107 Id. at 310.

108 Louis H. Pollak, ed., *The Constitution and the Supreme Court: A Documentary History*, 2 vols. (Cleveland and New York: The World Publishing Co., 1966).

109 Lincoln Caplan, Editorial, *New York Times*, 10 May 2012.